CONTENTS

Japanese Financial Policies
and the U.S. Trade Deficit

Introduction

The United States has a tradition of attributing its trade deficits to the financial policies of its major trading partners. The Nixon administration blamed the 1971 trade deficit on the failure of other industrial countries to revalue their currencies. The Carter administration blamed the large U.S. trade deficits in the latter half of the 1970s on the failure of Germany and Japan to undertake monetary and fiscal expansion. Blame for the rapidly rising U.S. trade and current-account deficits of the early 1980s has been assigned chiefly to the undervalued yen and to the Japanese financial policies to which it is attributed.

The emphasis on Japanese policies as a major cause of U.S. trade deficits is understandable. Despite some liberalization of Japan's imports, the U.S. bilateral trade deficit with Japan in 1984 was equal to almost a third of the total U.S. trade deficit, and the bilateral deficit with Japan in manufactured goods was over half the total U.S. deficit in manufactured goods (see Table 1 below). Therefore, it is generally believed that a large share of the increase in U.S. trade deficits from 1980 through 1984 can be attributed to Japan's trade and financial policies. The purpose of this essay is to examine the validity of this allegation with respect to Japan's financial policies.

The following criticisms of Japan's financial policies have been made:

1. Japan's intervention in the foreign-exchange markets has been biased toward depreciation of the yen in terms of the dollar.

2. Japan's mix of fiscal and monetary policies has contributed to an undervaluation of the yen.

3. Japan's high rate of personal savings combined with reduced domestic investment and restrictive fiscal policies have resulted in a surplus of domestic income over expenditures. This has given rise to large net capital exports, which in turn have depressed the exchange value of the yen.

4. Japan's control over international capital transactions and domestic capital markets and interest rates has encouraged capital exports, thereby contributing to the depreciation of the yen.

The authors appreciate the numerous helpful suggestions from Gary Saxonhouse, Robert E. Smith, Joe A. Stone, and an anonymous referee.

1

We first look at the changes in the U.S. and Japanese trade balances and exchange rates between 1980 and 1984. Next, we evaluate the above allegations as explanations for the increase in the U.S. multilateral trade deficit between 1980 and 1984. Finally, we examine the assumption implicit in these allegations that bilateral trade flows between the United States and Japan are sensitive to changes in the yen/dollar exchange rate. Because the focus is specifically on the role of Japan's financial policies in the growing U.S. trade deficit since 1980, we are not concerned with U.S. macroeconomic policies except as part of the total international environment for Japanese trade and financial relations. Nor are we concerned with the contribution of Japanese import barriers or export promotion to the U.S. trade deficit with Japan, about which there is considerable controversy.

Trade Balances and Exchange Rates

The Trade Balances

The total U.S. trade deficit has grown every year since 1980. In 1984 the United States had substantial trade deficits with every major trading partner or group, including Canada, the European Economic Community, Japan, the OPEC countries, and the oil-importing developing countries. In 1980, by contrast, the United States had a trade surplus with every major trading partner or group except Japan and the OPEC countries. In accounting for the large U.S. trade deficits, public attention has been centered on Japan, in part because the deficit with Japan has been larger than that with any other major trading partner and in part because of the high visibility of imports from Japan. In addition, U.S. exports of manufactures to Japan have been lower than to any other major trading partner and have averaged less than 20 percent of U.S. manufactured imports from Japan in recent years.

It is important to examine the U.S. trade balance with Japan in a historical context, because the trade balance in a given year reflects in part a structural trade relationship. The United States has had a bilateral trade deficit with Japan since 1965, and this deficit increased in most years from 1965 through 1984. It has also had a multilateral trade deficit in every year since 1975, and this deficit has increased in most years from 1975 through 1984. However, the proportion of the total trade deficit accounted for by the bilateral deficit with Japan declined from 48 percent in 1980 to 31 percent in 1984.

In every year from 1976 to 1982, the bilateral deficit with Japan on trade in manufactured goods was greater than the multilateral trade deficit in manufactured goods; in other words, the United States had a trade surplus in manufactured goods with the rest of the world, excluding Japan. But between 1980 and 1984 its multilateral trade deficit in manufactures grew by $97 billion (see Table 1), and in 1984 it had a $47 billion trade deficit in manufactures with the rest of the world, excluding Japan. Yet its bilateral manufacturing deficit with Japan increased by only $25 billion between 1980 and 1984, or by 35 percent of the deterioration in its trade balance in manufactures with the rest of the world, excluding Japan (see Table 1).

A striking element in the deterioration of the U.S. trade balance between 1980 and 1984 was the decline in total U.S. exports in the face of a 32 percent increase in total U.S. imports. U.S. exports hardly changed in current dollars but declined by about 17 percent in constant dollars. During this period,

TABLE 1

U.S. TRADE BALANCE

(in billions of current U.S. dollars)

	Total			Manufactured Goods [a]		
	U.S. Exports	U.S. Imports	Net Exports	U.S. Exports	U.S. Imports	Net Exports
U.S. Multilateral Trade						
1976	114.7	124.1	− 9.3	67.3	64.6	2.7
1977	120.8	151.7	− 30.9	69.6	76.9	− 7.3
1978	142.0	175.8	− 33.8	81.9	100.1	− 18.2
1979	184.5	211.8	− 27.3	99.4	110.9	− 11.6
1980	224.2	249.6	− 25.3	123.2	122.4	0.8
1981	237.0	256.1	− 28.1	133.1	139.1	− 6.0
1982	211.2	247.6	− 36.4	119.8	140.3	− 20.6
1983	200.7	262.8	− 62.1	112.7	159.3	− 46.6
1984	220.3	328.6	− 108.3	121.4	217.9	− 96.5
U.S.-Japanese Bilateral Trade						
1976	10.0	16.9	− 6.9	2.8	16.0	− 13.2
1977	10.4	20.3	− 9.9	2.8	19.2	− 16.5
1978	12.7	26.5	− 13.8	3.7	25.2	− 21.6
1979	17.4	28.2	− 10.8	5.2	26.8	− 21.5
1980	20.8	33.0	− 12.2	6.6	31.4	− 24.7
1981	21.8	39.9	− 18.1	7.2	38.1	− 31.0
1982	20.7	37.7	− 17.0	6.8	38.2	− 31.3
1983	21.7	41.3	− 19.6	7.5	41.5	− 34.0
1984	23.3	57.3	− 34.0	8.1	57.9	− 49.8

[a] Manufactures, machinery and transport equipment, and miscellaneous manufactures.

NOTE: Figures for total trade are f.o.b. Exports of manufactured goods are f.a.s., and imports are c.i.f. (Thus, imports of manufactured goods can be larger than total imports.)

SOURCE: *Survey of Current Business*, U.S. Department of Commerce, various issues; *Highlights of U.S. Exports and Import Trade*, U.S. Department of Commerce, various issues.

3

however, U.S. exports to Japan rose by 12 percent in current dollars and remained at about their 1980 level in constant dollars.

These data suggest that the change in the U.S.-Japanese trade balance between 1980 and 1984 was not the major contributing factor to the deterioration of the total U.S. trade balance. Although there was a large deterioration of the U.S. trade deficit in manufactured goods over the period, the bilateral balance with Japan performed relatively better than the balance with the rest of the world, excluding Japan.

Emphasis on Japan's large bilateral surplus with the United States can be misleading. In a multilateral trading system, structural factors make for large bilateral imbalances, and an increase in the overall surplus of one country may affect bilateral balances between other countries. We should therefore ask whether the growth in Japan's trade surplus between 1980 and 1984 was in part responsible for the deterioration of the U.S. trade balance with third countries. This could occur, for example, if Western Europe's manufactured exports to Japan were diverted to the United States as a consequence of increased Japanese import barriers. There is no evidence of such diversion, however. In 1984 Japan had a multilateral trade surplus of about $40 billion (f.o.b.), compared with $2 billion in 1980. But the dollar values of Japan's exports and imports in trade with Western Europe and the oil-importing developing countries were remarkably stable between 1980 and 1984. About 85 percent of the improvement in Japan's trade balance between 1980 and 1984 represents the improvement in its trade balance with the United States and the OPEC countries. Therefore, it seems unlikely that the increase in Japan's overall trade surplus contributed substantially to the deterioration in the U.S. trade balance with the rest of the world.

The Yen/Dollar Exchange Rate

Many observers hold that the yen has been undervalued and the dollar overvalued since 1980 (e.g., Bergsten, 1982a, and Williamson, 1983, p. 34). Although we question the economic significance of overvaluation or undervaluation with respect to exchange rates determined in free markets, we shall nevertheless examine evidence as to whether the yen was undervalued in a global context.

The value of the yen in terms of the dollar has fluctuated widely since 1976 (see Table 2). The yen reached its highest average level in terms of the dollar in 1978 but declined sharply thereafter, and by 1980 was 7 percent below its 1978 level; by 1982 it was 15 percent below that level. In 1983, however, the dollar value of the yen rose by 5 percent, and it maintained the same average level in 1984, remaining within 5 percent of its 1980 level (Table 2).

The effective yen exchange rate (trade-weighted against fifteen major currencies) appreciated by nearly 18 percent on a nominal basis between 1980

4

and 1984 (annual averages). The real effective yen rate depreciated by 5 percent between 1980 and 1984, but by less than the depreciation of the Deutschemark, the French franc, and the pound sterling. Among the currencies of America's major industrial trading partners, only the Canadian dollar appreciated in real terms during this period (see Table 2). It seems difficult, therefore, to make a case that the yen weakened on a global basis between 1980 and 1984.

Between 1980 and 1984, the purchasing power of the yen, measured by consumer prices, rose by 12.5 percent relative to that of the dollar, while the nominal yen/dollar rate declined by 4.6 percent. Hence, the exchange value of the yen in terms of the dollar was undervalued by about 17 percent in 1984 measured in terms of purchasing-power parity based on 1980. In these same terms, however, the Deutschemark and the pound sterling were undervalued in relation to the dollar by 43 and 36 percent respectively (1980 = 100). While we do not regard purchasing-power parity as a significant measure of

TABLE 2

NOMINAL AND REAL EFFECTIVE EXCHANGE RATES

(1980-82 average = 100)

	Yen/Dollar	Japan	U.S.	France	Germany	U.K.	Italy	Canada
Nominal:								
1976	78.3	78.3	100.8	113.8	85.2	91.3	138.5	123.5
1977	86.4	86.8	100.3	108.1	91.6	86.2	117.5	114.0
1978	110.3	106.9	92.1	106.4	88.7	86.2	118.2	104.0
1979	105.9	99.6	90.8	106.0	99.9	90.9	112.8	100.4
1980	102.4	95.5	90.7	106.5	100.0	99.8	108.4	100.4
1981	105.2	105.8	99.5	100.4	97.2	102.1	98.8	100.2
1982	93.2	98.6	109.8	93.1	102.8	98.1	92.8	99.4
1983	97.7	107.8	114.2	87.3	107.6	91.6	90.3	100.8
1984	97.7	113.0	122.4	84.4	107.4	88.1	86.7	97.3
Real:								
1976		98.3	94.7	103.8	104.7	70.6	102.3	116.2
1977		103.7	94.0	101.1	105.6	74.0	101.1	108.2
1978		118.5	88.3	100.7	106.0	77.1	98.6	100.3
1979		105.7	88.0	101.2	107.1	85.2	100.8	100.5
1980		103.1	89.5	102.2	103.5	99.2	103.5	99.6
1981		104.7	100.7	100.2	97.4	101.9	98.7	100.0
1982		92.3	109.8	97.7	99.1	98.9	97.8	100.4
1983		96.6	112.6	95.9	99.3	93.0	100.0	103.0
1984		97.6	118.1	96.4	96.5	89.2	100.9	101.2

NOTE: Effective exchange rate trade-weighted against fifteen major currencies.

SOURCE: *World Financial Markets* (April 1984 and April 1985), Morgan Guaranty Trust Company, and International Monetary Fund, various issues.

undervaluation, these calculations provide evidence for those who do that the yen did not depreciate relative to other major currencies.

Turning to another measure, Japan's "normalized" relative unit labor costs (i.e., unit labor costs adjusted for the real effective exchange rate and for cyclical swings), the index for Japan rose by 7 percent between 1980 and 1984. This rise was larger than that for all other major industrial countries except the United States and Canada, whose indexes rose by 43 and 17 percent respectively (*International Financial Statistics*, June 1985). In fact, the indexes for most industrial countries actually declined between 1980 and 1984. This suggests that Japanese unit labor costs have not declined relative to those of most other industrial countries. When measured in dollars, Japan's unit labor cost declined by 8 percent between 1980 and 1983, as contrasted with a rise of 11 percent for the United States. But this decline was smaller than those for other major U.S. trading partners, except Canada.

The various measures discussed above suggest that while the yen may have been undervalued in terms of the dollar in 1984, it was not undervalued in terms of other major currencies. All these measures are based on changes in the relationship between nominal exchange rates and relative prices or costs from a base period (1980) when the exchange value of the yen is assumed to have been more or less consistent with balance-of-payments equilibrium. But in the absence of strong exchange-market intervention leading to a large accumulation of official reserves, or of heavy trade and exchange restrictions, by what criterion should we judge whether the value of the yen was consistent with equilibrium in 1980 or was undervalued in 1984? To say a currency is undervalued simply on the basis of the current-account surplus is arbitrary if not meaningless.

For many years, economists defined equilibrium in terms of the basic balance: the sum of the current-account balance and net long-term capital flow. It is very difficult, however, to distinguish between short-term and long-term capital movements: financial instruments defined as long-term, such as bonds and stocks, are often held for short periods of time, so that transactions in long-term assets may be quite volatile. In recent years, efforts to define equilibrium have emphasized the relationship between "internal balance" and the current account. Internal balance usually refers to the relationship between domestic savings and domestic investment. Williamson (1983, p. 14) has sought to combine these two approaches by defining a "fundamental equilibrium exchange rate" as "that which is expected to generate a current account surplus or deficit equal to the underlying capital flow over the cycle, given that the country is pursuing 'internal balance' as best it can and not restricting trade for balance of payments reasons." But Williamson's definition is unsatisfactory both because of the difficulty of distinguishing between volatile and underlying capital movements and because there are no generally accepted

6

objective criteria for assessing the appropriateness of a country's "internal balance" as determined by domestic financial policies.

Japan's current-account surplus in 1984 was $35 billion, as contrasted with a current-account deficit of $11 billion in 1980. It has been argued that Japan's large surplus reflects a substantial degree of imbalance between domestic savings and investment that has given rise to portfolio shifts unrelated to real capital outflows. The nature of Japan's internal imbalance and its relationship to Japan's balance of payments will be examined below. Before taking up that subject, however, we will examine Japanese financial policies. In the absence of strong intervention in the exchange market, the exchange value of the yen is determined by the domestic policies of all major trading countries. Rather than ask whether the yen is undervalued, we therefore ask whether Japan's domestic financial policies are compatible with what may be regarded as a *desirable* framework for global balance-of-payments relationships.

Japanese Financial Policies

Japanese financial policies are believed to have reduced the exchange value of the yen and increased Japan's current-account surplus. These policies are said to include intervention in the foreign-exchange market, fiscal restraint combined with an expansionist monetary policy, and capital and credit controls that encourage capital exports. Japanese policies in each of these areas are examined in this section. It should be observed, however, that except for exchange-market intervention and direct controls over domestic and international financial transactions, the effects of domestic financial policies on the balance of payments of an individual country must be considered in the context of the financial policies of its major trading partners. In addition, they must be evaluated in relation to structural conditions within the country, such as the relationship between domestic savings and investment.

Intervention Policy

Some critics of Japanese policies, including spokesmen for the National Association of Manufacturers and the United Auto Workers (GAO, 1984, p. 38) have suggested that the Bank of Japan has pursued an intervention policy designed to maintain a relatively "low" yen value in order to promote Japan's export competitiveness. Testimony to this effect submitted to the Subcommittee on International Finance and Monetary Policy in its Hearings on Japanese-U.S. Trade in 1982 led the Subcommittee to request that the General Accounting Office undertake a study of Japanese foreign-exchange operations over the past ten years. The resulting report (GAO, 1984), as well as a number of other studies, do not support the view that Japanese intervention has systematically depressed the dollar value of the yen. The Bank of Japan's exchange-rate objectives have varied over the last decade. At times the Bank has defended a target rate, as in July 1978, when it sought to prevent the yen from rising above the ¥200-per-dollar level. However, the evidence suggests that the Bank's predominant policy has been "leaning against the wind."

Table 3 shows two measures of Japanese exchange-market intervention: gross changes in official Japanese reserves, and changes in the Japanese foreign-exchange-fund accounts.[1] Both measures show that the Bank of Japan has tended to buy yen when the yen is depreciating and sell yen when it is appreciating. For example, the 7.3 percent drop in the yen following the oil price shock in the fourth quarter of 1979 was met with heavy support operations by the Bank of Japan, as indicated by a $5 billion decline in official reserves and a decline of $6.2 billion in the foreign-exchange-funds account. In 1982 Japan lost almost $5 billion in reserves in an attempt to slow the decline in the yen against the dollar, while the foreign-exchange-funds measure that year shows that the Bank's intervention was even greater than the reserve loss: the Japanese authorities sold $8.9 billion (net) of foreign exchange. By contrast, during 1983 and the first quarter of 1984, a period when the yen was usually appreciating against the dollar, Japan acquired almost $2 billion in official reserves in order to moderate the appreciation.

Regression evidence derived from estimating intervention functions for the Bank of Japan also indicates that its policy was to lean against the wind. Argy (1982) estimated that the Bank of Japan bought or sold an average of $210 million in the current month in response to a 1 percent appreciation or depreciation in the effective trade-weighted value of the yen; his study covered the period March 1973 to December 1979. Similarly, Hutchison (1984) estimated that the Bank of Japan bought or sold approximately $167 million in the current month in response to a 1 percent appreciation or depreciation of the dollar value of the yen; this study covered the March 1973 to October 1981 period. Fried and Trezise (1983) argue that Japan moved to support the yen against the dollar in 1981-82, both by intervention in the foreign-exchange market and by restricting outflows of foreign capital.

While leaning against the wind may influence the exchange rate in the short term, this sort of intervention has little effect over extended periods; intervention on both sides of the market tends to cancel out. The intent of the

---

[1] The change in foreign-exchange funds differs from the corresponding change in gross international reserves by (1) including the change in official deposits of foreign exchange with commercial banks (the so-called "hidden reserves") and (2) excluding transactions that are conducted outside the foreign-exchange market. Including official Bank of Japan deposits of foreign exchange with commercial banks is useful. Upon occasion, Japan has used "hidden reserves" to conceal its spot foreign-exchange purchases by having a commercial bank buy or sell for the Bank of Japan in the commercial bank's name (Taylor, 1982, p. 70). The excluded extramarket transactions, comprised of earnings on official reserve assets and of receipts from U.S. military transactions, do not represent active Bank of Japan intervention.

TABLE 3

OFFICIAL JAPANESE INTERVENTION IN THE FOREIGN-EXCHANGE MARKET:
CHANGES IN RESERVES, FOREIGN-EXCHANGE FUNDS, AND EXCHANGE-RATE
(dollar figures in billions)

		Gross Change in Official Reserves (less gold) [a]	Change in the Foreign-Exchange Funds Account [b]	Percent Change in Yen/Dollar Exchange-Rate [c]
1974		$1.3	− $1.3	7.5%
1975		− 0.6	− 2.1	1.4
1976		3.8	2.6	− 4.0
1977		6.6	6.2	− 18.0
1978:	I	6.3	7.7	− 7.3
	II	− 1.9	1.1	− 7.9
	III	1.9	2.9	− 7.6
	IV	3.8	3.1	2.9
1979:	I	− 4.2	− 3.9	7.5
	II	− 4.1	− 4.1	3.7
	III	0.4	0.8	2.9
	IV	− 5.0	− 6.2	7.3
1980:	I	− 1.8	− 3.7	4.2
	II	4.1	2.4	− 12.8
	III	1.1	0.9	− 2.5
	IV	1.6	1.2	− 4.3
1981:	I	1.9	1.5	3.9
	II	1.0	0.3	7.0
	III	0.2	− 1.1	3.1
	IV	0.6	− 0.6	− 5.5
1982:	I	− 1.1	− 1.9	12.1
	II	− 1.7	− 2.6	3.0
	III	− 1.4	− 2.5	6.1
	IV	− 0.7	− 1.9	− 12.8
1983:	I	0.9	0.2	1.9
	II	0.9	0.1	0.1
	III	− 0.1	− 0.5	− 1.5
	IV	− 0.4	0.0	− 1.7
1984:	I	0.6	0.1	− 3.2
	II	0.1	− 0.5	5.7
	III	0.3	− 0.6	3.4
	IV	0.8	0.0	2.3

[a] *International Financial Statistics*, various issues.

[b] Bank of Japan, *Economic Statistics Monthly* (April 1985), Table 7. The flow of foreign-exchange funds is converted to dollars with period average yen/dollar exchange-rate data. Obtaining the dollar flow of funds by first differencing end-of-period outstanding stocks (after converting to dollars with end-of-period exchange-rate data) is not possible since end-of-period stock data are not available.

[c] Percent change in end-of-period yen/dollar exchange rates. Minus sign indicates appreciation of the yen.

9

policy is to slow but not reverse exchange-rate movements in the short run, in order to reduce exchange-rate volatility, while not interfering with longer-term trends. Admittedly, it is difficult to distinguish empirically between such behavior and episodes in which the Bank of Japan intended to hold the line on the yen but gave up when the cost became too great. Nonetheless, there is no evidence that the Bank has intervened systematically in recent years to depress the yen. Moreover, the scale of the Bank's intervention has been markedly smaller since 1983 than in previous years, as indicated in Table 3. The scale of the Bank's intervention and the size of Japan's foreign-exchange reserves are exceedingly small in relation to the total volume of transactions on the Japanese foreign-exchange market. In 1982, for example, the volume of Japanese interbank trading in all currencies totaled $1,285 billion, and direct yen/dollar trading was $1,186 billion (Hama, 1983, p. 27). By contrast, Japan's reserves totaled only $23 billion at the end of 1982.

The absence of a trend in the foreign-exchange portion of Japan's official reserves is further evidence that the Japanese authorities did not systematically intervene to depress the value of the yen. At the end of 1980, Japan's official foreign-exchange holdings totaled $21.6 billion, rising to $24.7 billion at the end of 1981, and declining to $19.2 billion at the end of 1982. At the end of 1984, they stood at $22.3 billion. The other components of Japan's reserves have either remained constant, as in the case of gold, or fluctuated passively in response to transactions initiated by others, as in the case of Japan's SDR holdings and reserve position in the IMF (*International Financial Statistics*, various issues).

Furthermore, Japan's official intervention in the foreign-exchange market is unlikely to have had a significant impact on the exchange rate because it has not been allowed to influence the monetary base—that is, intervention operations have been sterilized. This means that purchases or sales of foreign exchange by the central bank are accompanied by offsetting sales or purchases of domestic bonds, leaving the reserves of commercial banks unchanged. Nonsterilized intervention is likely to have a much greater effect on the exchange rate than sterilized intervention, because the former involves an increase or decrease in the domestic money supply, which in turn magnifies the effect on the exchange rate resulting from an official purchase or sale of foreign exchange.

Empirical evidence that the Bank of Japan routinely sterilizes its intervention operations is provided by estimates of the "sterilization coefficient." A sterilization coefficient equal to minus 1 indicates that the monetary base is totally insulated from the central bank's foreign-exchange operations. A coefficient equal to 0, by contrast, indicates that intervention is allowed to have its full effect on the money supply—official intervention is totally nonsteri-

10

lized. Two studies covering both the fixed- and floating-rate periods provide estimates of the sterilization coefficient for Japan: Hickman and Schleicher (1978) put it at -1.22 and Laney (1979) puts it at -1.69. Hutchison (1983) estimates the coefficient to be between -1.14 and -1.25 for the floating-rate period from October 1973 to October 1981. These estimates indicate that the Bank of Japan more than offsets the effects of its foreign-exchange purchases on the monetary base, that is, it reduces bank reserves by more than they are raised by foreign-exchange purchases. This evidence, together with *ex post* indications of leaning against the wind, suggests that the Bank's intervention operations have not consistently tended to depress the exchange value of the yen.

Monetary Policy

Under some circumstances, an expansionary monetary policy may promote capital exports. Therefore, it is important to consider the criticism that Japan's monetary policy was expansionary during the 1980-84 period (Bergsten, 1982b; *World Financial Markets*, December 1982, p. 6; *The Economist*, Nov. 19, 1983, p. 77). We examine several monetary indicators, including the rate of growth of the monetary aggregates, the rate of inflation, and changes in real interest rates.

After reducing the rate of monetary growth in response to the second oil price shock (1979-80), the Bank of Japan increased it in mid-1981 to between 9 and 10 percent per annum, as measured by M2 plus certificates of deposit— the most common monetary-growth measure in Japan—and it sharply decreased its discount rate (Yoshitomi, 1983b, p. 36). Thereafter, Japan's money growth rate declined. Despite a strong growth rate in real GNP, annual growth in M1 averaged 4.1 percent from 1982 through 1984, while the broader monetary aggregate, M2 plus CDs, rose at an average annual rate of 8.1 percent. By contrast, in the United States and Germany M1 grew at average annual rates of 8.2 and 7.2 percent respectively, while M2 grew at average annual rates of 9.9 and 5.7 percent respectively (*Economic Statistics Monthly*, Bank of Japan, April 1985, p. 182).

Perhaps the most significant indicator of monetary policy is the rate of inflation. Japan's inflation rate as measured by the CPI declined from nearly 8 percent in 1980 to 4.9 percent in 1981 and averaged less than 2.3 percent per year from 1982 through 1984. No other country has approached this record in recent years.

Movements in interest rates not only reflect monetary policy but may directly influence capital flows. Japan's nominal interest rates were significantly lower than those in the United States and most other industrial countries over most of the 1980-84 period. Only Germany and Switzerland had nominal in-

11

terest rates near or below those in Japan. Nevertheless, real short-term interest rates, that is, nominal rates less CPI inflation, have risen in Japan since 1981 and have not been low by international standards. They were below those of the United States and the United Kingdom in 1983 and 1984 but were generally above those of France, Germany, and Italy from 1981 to 1983 (see Table 4). The rise in Japan's real short-term interest rates after 1981 mainly reflected the decrease in the inflation rate rather than a rise in the nominal interest rate.

In recent years, the Bank of Japan has resisted domestic pressure to lower the discount rate and stimulate money growth, on the grounds that this would lead to a further depreciation of the yen (Hama, 1983, p. 34). From December 1981 to March 1985, it lowered its discount rate by only 50 basis points, and the 5 percent rate set in March 1983 has prevailed for more than two years. By contrast, the Federal Reserve lowered its discount rate from 12 percent in March 1981 to 8 percent in March 1985, while the Bundesbank lowered its discount rate from 7.5 to 4.5 percent over this same period. Of the major industrial countries, only France maintained an unchanged discount rate.

The OECD *Economic Survey, Japan* (1984, p. 26) observed that a key objective of monetary policy was to prevent a weakening of the external value of the yen, even though domestic economic conditions warranted greater monetary ease. Similarly, an international comparison of recent monetary policies concluded that the Bank of Japan has endeavored to limit depreciation of the yen by keeping interest rates higher than might have been desirable on do-

TABLE 4

REAL SHORT-TERM INTEREST RATES

	1981	1982	1983	1984
Japan	2.8	4.5	4.9	4.0
U.S.	6.0	6.1	5.9	5.9
France	1.9	2.9	3.0	4.6
Germany	5.8	3.6	2.5	3.6
U.K.	1.6	3.4	5.3	4.5
Italy	1.8	3.7	3.8	6.2
Canada	5.3	2.8	3.5	6.8

NOTE: Real interest rates are calculated as the difference between national money-market rates and CPI inflation.

SOURCE: *International Financial Statistics*, various issues. Money-market rates are derived from the following line items: U.S. and Italy (line 60b); Canada (60c); France, Japan, and Germany (60bs); and the U.K. (60cs). CPI inflation rate (64x).

mestic grounds (Atkinson and Chouraque, 1984, p. 28). Thus, there is substantial evidence that Japan has not followed an expansionary monetary policy in order to depress the yen.

Fiscal Policy

Although Japan cannot rightly be accused of pursuing an expansionary monetary policy during the 1982-84 period, it clearly adopted restrictive fiscal policies between 1979 and 1984. Moreover, there is widespread agreement that Japan's fiscal policy, pursued against a backdrop of high domestic savings and a relatively low level of domestic investment, has been a major cause of Japan's growing trade and current-account surpluses (Bergsten, 1982b; Saxonhouse, 1983; Yoshitomi, 1983a; OECD, 1984). Some economists in the Japanese Ministry of International Trade and Industry and in the Economic Planning Agency agree with this conclusion and have argued for a more stim-ulative fiscal policy in order to reduce the trade surplus. Economists in Japan's Ministry of Finance agree that Japanese "surplus saving" is an important cause of the large trade surplus but reject fiscal expansion as a cure. Rather, they argue that the government budget should be balanced by 1990 (*The Economist*, Apr. 27, 1985, p. 85). A reduction of budget deficits has been an objective of the Japanese government since 1979, when the cabinet announced its intention to eliminate the current deficit in the central government's budget by 1984 (Yoshitomi, 1983b, p. 36). A recent OECD report summarized current Japanese policy as "dominated by concern about large public sector deficits and the mounting volume of public debt" (OECD, 1984, p. 26).

There are two approaches to evaluating the impact of Japan's fiscal policies on international balance-of-payments equilibrium. One is to compare changes in Japan's fiscal policies with those of other major countries. This approach, which assumes that international equilibrium is promoted when major industrial nations follow similar financial policies, frequently underlies efforts to coordinate the financial policies of the major trading countries. The second approach is to evaluate Japan's fiscal policies in terms of basic internal variables, such as the rate of economic growth, unemployment, inflation, saving, and investment. We use both approaches.

Japan's central-government budget deficit rose as a percentage of GNP from 5.3 percent in 1978 to 6.0 percent in 1981 and then declined to 5.6 percent in 1984. By contrast, the U.S. Federal budget deficit rose from 2.2 percent of GNP in 1981 to 5.4 percent in 1983 and then fell to 4.8 percent in 1984. For five other major industrial countries, the trend in fiscal deficits was mixed. In Germany the central-government deficit fell from 2.2 percent of GNP in 1981 to 1.6 percent in 1984, and in the United Kingdom it fell from

13

4.1 percent to 3.3 percent. By contrast, the deficits of Canada, France, and Italy as percentages of GNP rose between 1981 and 1984 (*World Economic Outlook*, IMF, April 1985, p. 220). Although Japan has been pursuing a fiscal policy that is somewhat more restrictive than those of four of the six countries mentioned, its fiscal deficits in 1984 were larger as percentages of GNP than those of these countries except Canada and Italy. Overall, it does not appear that Japan's fiscal policy has been substantially out of step with those of other major industrial countries, excluding the United States.

Turning to the second approach, Japan has not pursued fiscal restraint at the expense of growth in real GNP, which has averaged about 4.3 percent from 1980 through 1984. Although its growth rate was higher during the 1970s, its 1980-84 rate was higher on average than that of any other major industrial country. Critics of Japan's fiscal policies have pointed out, however, that Japan has maintained a high rate of private saving, while its domestic investment has declined. Had Japan run larger fiscal deficits during the 1980-84 period, they argue, some of the "excess" private savings would have been absorbed domestically and less would have gone abroad in the form of capital exports.

From 1978 through 1980, fixed capital formation as a percentage of GNP averaged 31.6, while from 1983 through 1984, it averaged only 28.2 percent (*International Financial Statistics*, September 1985, p. 278). From 1978 through 1981, private savings in Japan (household plus corporate) were estimated at 29.3 percent of GNP, and private investment was estimated at 24.9 percent. But the excess of private savings over private investment was approximately offset by a fiscal deficit equal to 4.6 percent of GNP (Yoshitomi, 1983a, p. 20). In the 1980s, by contrast, private investment has been lower while private savings have remained at a relatively high level, estimated at nearly 30 percent of GNP in 1983. With the reduction in the fiscal deficit, there has been an excess of *overall* savings (private savings *less* the deficit) over private investment. This excess has been balanced by a growing current-account surplus (net foreign investment).

In view of the decline in private investment, should Japan have maintained or even increased its fiscal deficit to prevent a rise in its current-account surplus? The question raises two important issues.

First, given Japan's objective of reducing the fiscal deficit, are there other measures that might be used to reduce the current-account surplus? There are undoubtedly measures that the Japanese government could take to alter the country's savings and investment pattern without compromising its fiscal objective. For example, to discourage saving in favor of social expenditures, higher income taxes might be levied on large personal incomes and the proceeds devoted to housing subsidies and a variety of other social expenditures.

14

Greater use might also be made of investment tax credits. However, such changes might be even less acceptable to the government than a reversal of its policy on fiscal deficits.

The second issue has to do with the extent of Japan's responsibility for contributing to international balance. The large U.S. current-account deficit had to be offset somewhere by current-account surpluses. It has already been shown that Japan's trade balance reflects in the main the improvement in its trade balance with the OPEC countries and its trade surplus with the United States. How should responsibility between surplus and deficit countries be divided in the interest of international equilibrium?

Japan's responsibility for promoting international balance is set forth somewhat ambiguously by the OECD:

> The reduction of the public sector deficit may tend to increase net domestic saving, thereby maintaining upward pressure on current external transactions. Assuming no major imbalance in the OECD's global current-account position, a Japanese surplus of some size matched by net capital outflows should not be viewed as abnormal given the maturing of Japan's economy, her high saving propensity and her capacity to innovate. But in a context of high unemployment abroad and widespread protectionist sentiment, a number of conditions will have to be met for such a balance-of-payments pattern to be accepted internationally. Domestic demand in Japan must expand steadily and the exchange rate should be seen as properly reflecting the strength of fundamentals. But, equally important, the free operation of market forces in both goods and financial markets should not be hampered by remaining impediments of various sorts. (OECD, *Economic Surveys, Japan*, 1984, p. 67)

This report suggests that Japan has an international obligation to expand domestic demand, in addition to liberalizing trade and maintaining free internal and external financial markets. But the Japanese authorities might well take the position that an expansion of domestic demand in the face of relatively low unemployment and satisfactory economic growth would increase the inflation rate, and that the major responsibility for restoring international balance lies with the countries experiencing current-account deficits, mainly the United States. This is an old issue that was debated during the pre-Bretton Woods discussions in Washington and again in 1970-71 when the U.S. Treasury was putting pressure on European members of the IMF to appreciate their currencies and adopt expansionary financial policies. In one form or another, it is the old question of whether surplus countries as well as deficit countries have an obligation to adjust their financial policies.

Liberalization of Financial Markets

Japanese controls over domestic and international capital transactions have been regarded as promoting net capital outflows and thereby tending to weaken the yen in the exchange markets (*The Economist*, Nov. 19, 1983, p. 77; Murchison and Soloman, 1983). This belief was expressed by the U.S. Secretary of the Treasury, Donald Regan, at the American Center in Tokyo on March 24, 1985: "Why is the yen weak in relation to the dollar when there is an imbalance in trade [in Japan's favor]? It is because the yen is a protected currency and the dollar is free." Secretary Regan's statement was a gross exaggeration, since Japan had already taken a number of important steps to liberalize its capital markets. Furthermore, it would be difficult to determine whether the remaining controls tend on balance to strengthen or weaken the yen. Nevertheless, following negotiations with U.S. Treasury officials in May 1984, Japan's Minister of Finance agreed to accelerate the liberalization of Japanese financial markets and the internationalization of the yen.

Prior to the late 1970s, Japan maintained a variety of restrictions on both imports and exports of capital. Beginning in the late 1970s and continuing during the 1980s, controls on both foreign and domestic capital markets were relaxed or removed. The Foreign Exchange and Foreign Trade Control Law of December 1980 officially confirmed the process of financial liberalization that had been taking place in Japan at the administrative level. The importance of the law was more than technical, given the considerable delays Japanese and foreign institutions often encounter in Japan in obtaining official approval for their actions (Pigott, 1983, p. 40). The 1980 law also established the principle that all international transactions would be free of controls, thereby reversing the old principle of prohibiting transactions unless specifically authorized by the authorities (Wakatsuki, 1984, p. 3). In practice, however, the Japanese Ministry of Finance has continued to oversee, and at times restrict, volume and market access in certain categories of transactions. Controls continue to be exercised on overseas syndicated lending, foreign participation in the Japanese securities market, the Euroyen securities market, and purchases of foreign securities by Japanese institutional investors (Freeman, 1984, p. 8).

Nevertheless, there has been considerable liberalization of Japan's international transactions, and it has taken place more rapidly than deregulation of domestic capital markets. Although some progress has been made in freeing interest rates, rates for bank deposits and bank lending are not fully determined by market forces (Freeman, 1984, p. 9).

The deregulation of Japanese financial markets in recent years appears to have spurred capital outflows independently of the incentives provided by higher interest rates abroad. Japanese residents and institutions have for the first time been given an opportunity to diversify their portfolios by acquiring foreign assets. A substantial part of the recent increase in recorded capital outflows may therefore reflect a gradual but one-time stock adjustment. Thus

16

far, capital inflows have not increased as much as outflows in response to liberalization measures. But financial markets in Japan are still relatively undeveloped and offer only a limited range of financial instruments to foreign investors. As the number and variety of financial markets expand, larger amounts of foreign capital should be drawn to Japan.

Because international capital liberalization is proceeding somewhat in advance of domestic liberalization, net capital outflows may have been temporarily promoted. Yet the capital restrictions that remain pertain largely to capital outflows. This observation is consistent with the testimony of Bergsten (1984, p. 4) that "the recently announced 'U.S.-Japan yen agreement' will make the problem worse at least in the short run, by encouraging more capital outflow from Japan."

The Yen/Dollar Exchange Rate and U.S. Trade with Japan

Between 1980 and 1984 the U.S. bilateral trade deficit with Japan increased from $12 to $34 billion, or nearly threefold, and the bilateral deficit in manufactured goods approximately doubled. In the previous section, we explored four Japanese financial policies that have been offered as fundamental explanations for these increases—systematic intervention in the yen/dollar market, expansionary monetary policy, restrictive fiscal policy, and capital controls. In each case, we asked whether the policy had led to the deterioration in the U.S. trade balance with Japan by causing a sustained depreciation in the dollar value of the yen.

In principle, however, a change in the exchange rate may have a strong or weak effect on the trade balance between two countries. As Magee (1973) pointed out, the effect depends on two factors—the pricing behavior of exporters in response to a change in the exchange rate, called "passthrough," and the behavior of importers in response to a change in the prices of traded goods. Different trade-balance effects are implied by alternative patterns of passthrough and differing price elasticities of demand. One such effect that has been discerned in some research is the J-curve, when depreciation of a country's currency initially impairs its trade balance but improves it over time.[2]

This section surveys previous empirical work on the sensitivity of U.S. trade with Japan to movements in the exchange rate. It examines estimates of

[2] The reason for a J-curve is twofold—depreciation tends to increase import prices more rapidly than export prices (in the domestic currency), so that passthrough is more rapid on the import side, and demand responds to price changes with a lag of several quarters. The conventional wisdom about the time pattern of the J-curve is that improvement in the trade balance occurs one to two years after depeciation (Goldstein and Young, 1979).

price elasticities of demand and of passthrough patterns in supply for Japanese multilateral trade and for bilateral trade between the two countries. The section concludes with an assessment of the implications of an appreciation of the yen.

Japanese Multilateral Evidence

The vast majority of empirical studies on exchange-rate effects are multilateral in nature, but they throw some light on bilateral effects as well. Because over a third of Japanese exports go to the United States, the sensitivity of bilateral trade between them can be obtained indirectly from estimates measuring the response of Japanese multilateral trade to changes in the foreign-currency value of the yen. In addition, multilateral evidence may provide some information about competition from third markets.

The price sensitivity of the foreign demand for Japanese exports has been shown in most studies to be strong, at the aggregate and disaggregated levels. In the survey by Stern, Francis, and Schumacher (1976, p. 21), the "best" point estimates for the long-run price elasticity of foreign demand for total Japanese exports and for manufactured exports are -1.77 and -1.24 respectively. The price sensitivity of Japan's demand for imports has been found to be weaker than for exports, especially for total imports. In Stern *et al.* (1976, p. 21), the best point estimate for the long-run elasticity of the Japanese for imports is -1.42 for manufactured imports but only -0.78 for total imports, each less than the corresponding estimate for exports. The finding of higher price elasticities of demand for exports than for imports seems reasonable. Price elasticities of demand for manufactured goods are consistently higher than for other categories (Stern *et al.*, 1976, p. 13), and the bulk of Japanese exports are in manufactured goods, whereas the bulk of Japanese imports are primary products and industrial materials.

The second factor determining exchange-rate effects on trade is the pricing behavior of exporters. Recent estimates (Spitaller, 1980; Bernauer, 1981; and Citrin, 1985) find passthrough to be about 50 percent for Japanese exports but close to 100 percent for Japanese imports, implying a stronger exchange-rate effect on imports. The survey by Goldstein and Khan (1985, p. 1090) reports a similar finding, and they argue that the stronger passthrough on the import side helps to explain the early stages of the J-curve found in the response of the Japanese trade balance.

The net effect of exchange-rate changes on Japanese trade based on these partial-equilibrium studies and on major econometric models has been found to be strong. As summarized by Saxonhouse (1983, pp. 279-280), "a change in the price of the yen relative to other currencies will result in a substantial change in the Japanese current account," an implication of all models pertain-

18

ing to Japan "regardless of the detail or the lack of detail in their treatment of the foreign sector and its linkages with the domestic economy and abroad."

Recent studies of Japan that include data after 1980, however, question this optimistic finding. Using a model that allows for the effect of changes in final demand on imported inputs, Ueda (1983) finds that a change in the value of the yen does not have very large effects on Japan's trade balance in the short or long run. Citrin (1985) presents detailed estimates for five of Japan's export industries and finds significant price effects on demand for only two of them. Finally, Turner and Tuveri (1984) find weak exchange-rate effects on Japanese exports, because of both low price elasticities of demand and incomplete passthrough. They attribute their findings to the voluntary export quotas adopted by Japan, which became significant after 1979.

U.S.-Japanese Bilateral Evidence

There have been a few estimates of bilateral trade models, which attempt to hold third-country effects constant. Earlier studies of bilateral trade between the United States and Japan have generally found that the price elasticity of U.S. demand for imports from Japan is strong and at least as large as the elasticity of Japanese demand for imports from the United States (Houthakker and Magee, 1969; Price and Thornblade, 1972). This finding is consistent with the Japanese multilateral evidence prior to 1980. However, bilateral estimates that include data after 1980 indicate that U.S. imports from Japan are not highly responsive to exchange-rate movements. Using quarterly data on trade in manufactured goods from the fourth quarter of 1974 to the first quarter of 1983, Haynes, Hutchison, and Mikesell (1986) have made reduced-form estimates that show a strong effect on the value of U.S. exports to Japan of a change in the yen/dollar exchange rate but essentially no effect on U.S. imports from Japan. Our structural estimates explain this difference in responsiveness. For U.S. exports to Japan, the supply equation indicates complete passthrough after one year, and the demand equation has a large long-run exchange-rate elasticity of -4.40. For U.S. imports from Japan, the supply equation indicates significant but incomplete passthrough even in the steady state, and the demand equation has a long-run elasticity that is quite low (-0.43) and not statistically significant. The weakness in the response of U.S. imports from Japan, because of both incomplete passthrough and an inelastic demand, conforms with the findings of Turner and Tuveri (1984) regarding Japan's multilateral exports.[3]

---

[3] Although we attribute the reduced exchange-rate sensitivity of U.S. imports from Japan to the inclusion of post-1980 data, the use of different structural models with alternative methods of capturing lagged adjustment may also provide a partial explanation.

Reduced price sensitivity for Japanese exports in recent years is consistent with the fact that some of these exports have been subject to market restraints. For example, the bilateral agreement concluded with the United States in May 1977 limited Japanese exports of color television sets for a three-year period. In April 1978, eight industries, including automobiles, were subjected to intensified monitoring and guidance. Formal voluntary export restraints on passenger automobiles went into effect on April 1, 1981. They have been renewed annually through March 31, 1986, although the 1985-86 restraints are less severe because the ceiling was raised by 25 percent. These and other restraints no doubt inhibited additional Japanese exporters from exploiting their competitive edge. Taken together, the various explicit and implicit restraints have severely limited a wide variety of Japanese exports since about 1980 (Turner and Tuveri, 1984, p. 96). Theory predicts that effective quotas reduce quantities, may increase prices, and will cause demand to appear insensitive to price and income changes. The recent reduction in the price sensitivity of demand for Japanese exports found by Turner and Tuveri (1984) and by Haynes, Hutchison, and Mikesell (1986) seems best explained by this phenomenon.

Although passthrough is usually found to be incomplete on the export side for most countries (Spitaller, 1980), there are at least two reasons why Japanese exporters in particular may have been reluctant in recent years to pass through exchange-rate changes fully in the form of lower dollar prices to U.S. customers. First, if Japanese exporters believed the yen depreciation that began in 1978 was going to be temporary, they probably preferred to accept temporary profits rather than expand production to increase their market shares in the United States, because subsequent yen appreciation would have reduced their profits. Anecdotal evidence supports this supposition. *Business Week* (January 1984, p. 42) reports that since 1980 many Japanese exporters have "quietly streamlined their operations to be efficient and profitable even if their currency strengthens to 200 to the dollar." It quotes Sozaburo Okamatsu, of the Ministry of International Trade and Industry, as saying that "many major exporters began adjusting internally for an anticipated exchange rate of 200 yen to the dollar back in 1980." Comments by executives of McKinsey and Company, Sony, Victor, and Fujitsu also describe such behavior.

A second possible explanation for incomplete passthrough is that the United States would probably retaliate with further trade restrictions if Japanese exporters passed through the whole of the yen depreciation in the form of lower dollar prices in order to increase their market shares.

Furthermore, with voluntary quotas on exports, reductions in dollar prices would not increase market shares but only reduce dollar revenues.

Implications for Yen Appreciation

Since trade in manufactured goods is in principle the only sort that should be sensitive to exchange-rate movements in the short and intermediate run, and since U.S. imports of manufactured goods from Japan have have been six times as large during the last decade as exports of manufactured goods to Japan, the sensitivity of U.S. bilateral trade with Japan to changes in the yen/dollar rate must depend primarily on the behavior of U.S. imports. The evidence presented above indicates that U.S. imports from Japan were strongly sensitive to exchange-rate movements during the 1960s and 1970s but that, from data after 1980, this may no longer be true, apparently because of market restraints. This finding does *not* rule out the possibility that the yen depreciation that began in 1978 contributed to the deterioration of the U.S. trade balance between 1980 and 1984. The restraints were imposed in the first place and became effective in limiting volume because of the strong U.S. demand for Japanese goods, no doubt caused in part by the weakening yen. The volume, and possibly the value, of U.S. imports from Japan would have been larger from 1980 through 1984 in the absence of these restraints. It does imply, however, that a yen appreciation will not necessarily improve the U.S. trade balance with Japan now that the restraints are in place.

If this analysis is correct, a change in Japanese financial policies causing a sustained appreciation of the yen may not dramatically reduce the U.S. trade deficit with Japan in the intermediate run. With incomplete passthrough, a yen appreciation leads to only a partial increase in the dollar prices of U.S. imports from Japan. Even if there is a significant increase in their dollar prices, moreover, the volume of imports will not decline so long as the restraints are effective. Only when the appreciation of the yen has reduced the U.S. demand for Japanese goods below the point at which the restraints are effective will it be possible for the volume and thus the value of these imports to decrease.

Conclusions

How important has the U.S. trade deficit with Japan been to the deterioration of the overall U.S. trade deficit since 1980? In 1984 the bilateral trade deficit of the United States with Japan and the corresponding trade deficit in manufactured goods represented 34 and 52 percent respectively of its multilateral trade and manufactured-goods deficits. But this observation is misleading. The United States has had a bilateral trade deficit with Japan since 1965, and this deficit has increased in most years over the 1965-84 period. However, the

21

proportion of the U.S. multilateral deficit accounted for by the U.S. deficit with Japan *declined* from 48 percent in 1980 to 31 percent in 1984.

While the importance of the U.S. trade deficit with Japan should not be discounted, any analysis of the factors contributing to the growth of the overall U.S. trade deficit during the 1980s must consider the structural factors in U.S. trade with Japan. A structural trade imbalance between the two countries has existed for nearly two decades, and it cannot readily be reduced by an alteration in Japan's financial policies. Even a substantial policy change leading to a reduction in Japan's overall trade surplus is likely to leave a large U.S. trade deficit with Japan.

Our analysis of the contribution of Japan's financial policies to the increase in the U.S. trade deficit with Japan between 1980 and 1984 yields mixed conclusions.

First, we find little evidence to support the charge that the Bank of Japan deliberately depressed the exchange rate of the yen by means of intervention in the exchange market. Rather, the Bank of Japan generally followed a policy of leaning against the wind.

Second, Japan does not appear to have followed an expansionary monetary policy—a policy that would have depressed the yen.

Third, there was a steady decline in the ratio of Japan's government budget deficit to GNP between 1978 and 1984, indicating a policy of fiscal restraint. There was also a substantial decline in fixed investment as a percentage of GNP over this period, as well as evidence that private savings as a percentage of GNP either did not decline or fell by less than the decrease in investment. Thus the decrease in the fiscal deficit tended to create an excess of private savings over net domestic investment, and this excess was reflected in Japan's growing current-account surplus and net capital outflow.

Fourth, Japan has been liberalizing domestic financial markets, as well as international capital transactions. The net impact on capital flows may depend on the timing of various portions of the liberalization program. Since international capital liberalization has tended to proceed somewhat faster than domestic financial liberalization, the overall program probably promoted net capital outflow.

Our review of empirical studies on the sensitivity of Japan's trade balances to changes in the exchange rate shows that U.S. imports from Japan were relatively insensitive to changes in the dollar value of the yen after 1979. In large part, the explanation is that a wide variety of Japanese exports to the United States have been subject to voluntary export controls during the 1980s. This finding has implications for the potential effects of an appreciation of the yen on the U.S. trade balance with Japan. An appreciation might simply render the voluntary export controls redundant without substantially reducing U.S. imports from Japan. Although an appreciation of the yen would be expected

22

to increase U.S. exports of manufactures to Japan, such exports represented only 13 percent of U.S. imports of manufactures from Japan in 1984.

In summary, of the four Japanese financial policies examined, only the reduction in the fiscal deficit, against a background of reduced domestic investment and high private savings, can be regarded as having contributed significantly to Japan's growing trade surplus and the depreciation of the dollar value of the yen. Furthermore, because of Japan's voluntary export controls and the structural imbalance of U.S. trade with Japan, an appreciation of the dollar value of the yen in response to a change in Japan's financial policies is unlikely to result in a substantial decrease in the U.S. trade deficit with Japan.

References

Argy, Victor, *Exchange-Rate Management in Theory and Practice*, Essays in International Finance No. 50, Princeton, N.J., Princeton University, International Finance Section, 1982.

Atkinson, Paul, and Jean-Claude Chouraque, *The Conduct of Monetary Policy in the Current Recovery*, OECD Working Papers No. 14, Paris, Economics and Statistics Department, 1984.

Bergsten, C. Fred, "What to Do about the U.S.-Japan Economic Conflict," *Foreign Affairs*, 60 (Summer 1982a), pp. 1054-1075.

———, "What to Do about Japan?" address to the Japan Society, New York, May 5, 1982b.

———, "The United States Trade Deficit and the Dollar," *Hearings before Senate Subcommittee on International Finance and Monetary Policy*, Washington, June 6, 1984.

Bernauer, Kenneth, "Effectiveness of Exchange-Rate Changes on the Trade Account: The Japanese Case," *Economic Review of the Federal Reserve Bank of San Francisco* (Fall 1981), pp. 55-71.

Citrin, Daniel, "Exchange Rate Changes and Japanese Exports of Selected Industries," *IMF Staff Papers*, 32 (September 1985), pp. 404-429.

Economic Survey of Japan, Tokyo, Japanese Planning Agency, 1980/81.

Frankel, Jeffrey A., *The Yen-Dollar Agreement: Liberalizing Japanese Capital Markets*, Washington, Institute for International Economics, 1984.

Freeman, Richard, "Aspects of Recent Japanese Financial Market Liberalization," discussion paper presented to Committee on Asian Economic Studies of the Federal Reserve Bank of San Francisco, May 11, 1984.

Fried, E. R., and P. H. Trezise, "An Introductory Perspective," in *The Future Course of U.S.-Japan Economic Relations*, Washington, The Brookings Institution, 1983, pp. 1-6.

General Accounting Office, *Floating Exchange Rates in an Interdependent World: No Simple Solutions to the Problems*, Washington, Apr. 20, 1984.

Goldstein, Morris, and Mohsin S. Khan, "Income and Price Effects in International Trade," in Ronald W. Jones and Peter B. Kenen, eds., *Handbook of International Economics, Vol. II*, Amsterdam, Elsevier, 1985, pp. 1041-1105.

Goldstein, Morris, and John Young, "Exchange Rate Policy: Some Current Issues," *Finance and Development*, 16 (March 1979), pp. 7-10.

Hama, Atsushi, *The Yen-Dollar Relationship, Macro-Economic Policy, Financial and Capital Markets, and Related Issues*, Keidanren Papers No. 10, Tokyo, 1983.

Haynes, Stephen E., Michael M. Hutchison, Raymond F. Mikesell, "U.S.-Japanese Bilateral Trade and the Yen-Dollar Exchange Rate: An Empirical Analysis," *Southern Economic Journal*, 52 (April 1986).

Hickman, G. B., and S. Schleicher, "The Interdependence of National Economies and the Synchronization of Economic Fluctuations: Evidence from the LINK Project," *Weltwirtschaftliches Archiv*, 4 (1978), pp. 642-708.

Houthakker, Hendrik S., and Stephen P. Magee, "Income and Price Elasticities in World Trade," *Review of Economics and Statistics*, 64 (1969), pp. 111-125.

Hutchison, Michael M., "Impact of Central Bank Intervention on Exchange Rate Movements: Case of Japan, 1973-82," Eugene, Oreg., University of Oregon, 1983, unpublished Ph.D. dissertation.

———, "Official Japanese Intervention in Foreign Exchange Markets: Leaning Against the Wind?" *Economics Letters*, 15 (1984), pp. 115-120.

Laney, L. O., "National Monetary Independence in Managed Floating Exchange Rates," Research Paper No. 7905, Dallas, Federal Reserve Bank, 1979.

Magee, Stephen P., "Currency Contracts, Pass-through, and Devaluation," *Brookings Papers on Economic Activity*, 1 (1973), pp. 303-3256.

Murchison, David C., and Ezra Soloman, "The Misalignment of the United States Dollar and the Japanese Yen: The Problem and Its Solution," Sept. 19, 1983, unpublished.

Organization for Economic Cooperation and Development, "Japan," *Economic Surveys 1982/3*, Paris, July 1984.

Pigott, Charles, "Financial Reform in Japan," *Economic Review of the Federal Reserve Bank of San Francisco* (Winter 1983), pp. 25-46.

Price, James E., and James B. Thornblade, "U.S. Import Demand Functions Disaggregated by Country and Commodity," *Southern Economic Journal*, 39 (July 1972), pp. 46-67.

Saxonhouse, Gary R., "The Micro- and Macroeconomics of Foreign Sales to Japan," in William R. Cline, ed., *Trade Policy for the 1980s*, Cambridge, Mass., MIT Press, 1983, pp. 259-304.

Spitaller, Erich, "Short-Run Effects of Exchange Rate Changes on Terms of Trade and Trade Balances," *IMF Staff Papers*, 27 (June 1980), pp. 320-348.

Stern, Robert M., Jonathon Francis, and Bruce Schumacher, *Price Elasticities in International Trade*, London, Macmillan, 1976.

Taylor, Dean, "The Mismanaged Float: Official Intervention by the Industrialized Countries," in Michael B. Connolly, *The International Monetary System: Choices for the Future*, New York, Praeger, 1982.

Turner, Philip, and Jean-Pierre Tuveri, "Some Effects of Export Restraints on Japanese Trading Behavior," *OECD Economic Studies*, 2 (Spring 1984), pp. 93-107.

Ueda, Kazuo, "Trade Balance Adjustment with Imported Intermediate Goods: The Japanese Case," *Review of Economics and Statistics*, 65 (1983), pp. 618-625.

Wakatsuki, Mikio, "Internationalization of the Tokyo Financial Markets: Economic Implication," discussion paper presented to Committee on Asian Economic Studies of the Federal Reserve Bank of San Francisco, May 11, 1984.

Williamson, John, *The Exchange Rate System*, Washington, Institute for International Economics, 1983.

Yoshitomi, Masaru, "An Analysis of Current-Account Surpluses in the Japanese Economy," in *The Future Course of U.S.-Japan Economic Relations*, Washington, The Brookings Institution, 1983a, pp. 9-24.

———, "An Appraisal of Japanese Financial Policies," *World Economy*, 6 (1983b), pp. 27-38.

PUBLICATIONS OF THE
INTERNATIONAL FINANCE SECTION

Notice to Contributors

The International Finance Section publishes at irregular intervals papers in four series: ESSAYS IN INTERNATIONAL FINANCE, PRINCETON STUDIES IN INTERNATIONAL FINANCE, SPECIAL PAPERS IN INTERNATIONAL ECONOMICS, and REPRINTS IN INTERNATIONAL FINANCE. ESSAYS and STUDIES are confined to subjects in international finance. SPECIAL PAPERS are surveys of the literature suitable for courses in colleges and universities.

An ESSAY should be a lucid exposition of a theme, accessible not only to the professional economist but to other interested readers. It should therefore avoid technical terms, should eschew mathematics and statistical tables (except when essential for an understanding of the text), and should rarely have footnotes.

A STUDY or SPECIAL PAPER may be more technical. It may include statistics and algebra and may have many footnotes. STUDIES and SPECIAL PAPERS may also be longer than ESSAYS; indeed, these two series are meant to accommodate manuscripts too long for journal articles and too short for books.

To facilitate prompt evaluation, please submit three copies of your manuscript. Retain one for your files. The manuscript should be typed on one side of 8½ by 11 strong white paper. All material should be double-spaced—text, excerpts, footnotes, tables, references, and figure legends. For more complete guidance, prospective contributors should send for the Section's style guide before preparing their manuscripts.

How to Obtain Publications

A mailing list is maintained for free distribution of all new publications to college, university, and public libraries and nongovernmental, nonprofit research institutions.

Individuals and organizations not qualifying for free distribution can obtain ESSAYS and REPRINTS as issued and announcements of new STUDIES and SPECIAL PAPERS by paying a fee of $12 (within U.S.) or $15 (outside U.S.) to cover the period January 1 through December 31, 1986. Alternatively, for $30 they can receive all publications automatically—SPECIAL PAPERS and STUDIES as well as ESSAYS and REPRINTS.

ESSAYS and REPRINTS can also be ordered from the Section at $2.50 per copy, and STUDIES and SPECIAL PAPERS at $4.50. Payment MUST be included with the order and MUST be made in U.S. dollars. PLEASE INCLUDE $1 FOR POSTAGE AND HANDLING. (These charges are waived on orders from persons or organizations in countries whose foreign-exchange regulations prohibit such remittances.) For airmail delivery outside U.S., Canada, and Mexico, there is an additional charge of $1.

All manuscripts, correspondence, and orders should be addressed to:

International Finance Section
Department of Economics, Dickinson Hall
Princeton University
Princeton, New Jersey 08544

Subscribers should notify the Section promptly of a change of address, giving the old address as well as the new one.

List of Recent Publications

Some earlier issues are still in print. Write the Section for information.

ESSAYS IN INTERNATIONAL FINANCE

130. Franco Modigliani and Tommaso Padoa-Schioppa, *The Management of an Open Economy with "100% Plus" Wage Indexation*. (Dec. 1978)
131. H. Robert Heller and Malcolm Knight, *Reserve-Currency Preferences of Central Banks*. (Dec. 1978)
132. Robert Triffin, *Gold and the Dollar Crisis: Yesterday and Tomorrow*. (Dec. 1978)
133. Herbert G. Grubel, *A Proposal for the Establishment of an International Deposit Insurance Corporation*. (July 1979)
134. Bertil Ohlin, *Some Insufficiencies in the Theories of International Economic Relations*. (Sept. 1979)
135. Frank A. Southard, Jr., *The Evolution of the International Monetary Fund*. (Dec. 1979)
136. Niels Thygesen, *Exchange-Rate Experiences and Policies of Small Countries: Some European Examples in the 1970s*. (Dec. 1979)
137. Robert M. Dunn, Jr., *Exchange Rates, Payments Adjustments, and OPEC: Why Oil Deficits Persist*. (Dec. 1979)
138. Tom de Vries, *On the Meaning and Future of the European Monetary System*. (Sept. 1980)
139. Deepak Lal, *A Liberal International Economic Order: The International Monetary System and Economic Development*. (Oct. 1980)
140. Pieter Korteweg, *Exchange-Rate Policy, Monetary Policy, and Real Exchange-Rate Variability*. (Dec. 1980)
141. Bela Balassa, *The Process of Industrial Development and Alternative Development Strategies*. (Dec. 1980)
142. Benjamin J. Cohen, *The European Monetary System: An Outsider's View*. (June 1981)
143. Marina v. N. Whitman, *International Trade and Investment: Two Perspectives*. (July 1981)
144. Sidney Dell, *On Being Grandmotherly: The Evolution of IMF Conditionality*. (Oct. 1981)
145. Ronald I. McKinnon and Donald J. Mathieson, *How to Manage a Repressed Economy*. (Dec. 1981)
*146. Bahram Nowzad, *The IMF and Its Critics*. (Dec. 1981)
147. Edmar Lisboa Bacha and Carlos F. Díaz Alejandro, *International Financial Intermediation: A Long and Tropical View*. (May 1982)
148. Alan A. Rabin and Leland B. Yeager, *Monetary Approaches to the Balance of Payments and Exchange Rates*. (Nov. 1982)
149. C. Fred Bergsten, Rudiger Dornbusch, Jacob A. Frenkel, Steven W. Kohlhagen, Luigi Spaventa, and Thomas D. Willett, *From Rambouillet to Versailles: A Symposium*. (Dec. 1982)

150. Robert E. Baldwin, *The Inefficacy of Trade Policy*. (Dec. 1982)
151. Jack Guttentag and Richard Herring, *The Lender-of-Last Resort Function in an International Context*. (May 1983)
152. G. K. Helleiner, *The IMF and Africa in the 1980s*. (July 1983)
153. Rachel McCulloch, *Unexpected Real Consequences of Floating Exchange Rates*. (Aug. 1983)
154. Robert M. Dunn, Jr., *The Many Disappointments of Floating Exchange Rates*. (Dec. 1983)
155. Stephen Marris, *Managing the World Economy: Will We Ever Learn?* (Oct. 1984)
156. Sebastian Edwards, *The Order of Liberalization of the External Sector in Developing Countries*. (Dec. 1984)
157. Wilfred J. Ethier and Richard C. Marston, eds., with Kindleberger, Guttentag and Herring, Wallich, Henderson, and Hinshaw, *International Financial Markets and Capital Movements: A Symposium in Honor of Arthur I. Bloomfield*. (Sept. 1985)
158. Charles E. Dumas, *The Effects of Government Deficits: A Comparative Analysis of Crowding Out*. (Oct. 1985)
159. Jeffrey A. Frankel, *Six Possible Meanings of "Overvaluation": The 1981-85 Dollar*. (Dec. 1985)
160. Stanley W. Black, *Learning from Adversity: Policy Responses to Two Oil Shocks*. (Dec. 1985)
161. Alexis Rieffel, *The Role of the Paris Club in Managing Debt Problems*. (Dec. 1985)
162. Stephen E. Haynes, Michael M. Hutchison, Raymond F. Mikesell, *Japanese Financial Policies and the U.S. Trade Deficit*. (April 1986)

PRINCETON STUDIES IN INTERNATIONAL FINANCE

44. Clas Wihlborg, *Currency Risks in International Financial Markets*. (Dec. 1978)
45. Ian M. Drummond, *London, Washington, and the Management of the Franc, 1936-39*. (Nov. 1979)
46. Susan Howson, *Sterling's Managed Float: The Operations of the Exchange Equalisation Account, 1932-39*. (Nov. 1980)
47. Jonathan Eaton and Mark Gersovitz, *Poor Country Borrowing in Private Financial Markets and the Repudiation Issue*. (June 1981)
48. Barry J. Eichengreen, *Sterling and the Tariff, 1929-32*. (Sept. 1981)
49. Peter Bernholz, *Flexible Exchange Rates in Historical Perspective*. (July 1982)
50. Victor Argy, *Exchange-Rate Management in Theory and Practice*. (Oct. 1982)
51. Paul Wonnacott, *U.S. Intervention in the Exchange Market for DM, 1977-80*. (Dec. 1982)
52. Irving B. Kravis and Robert E. Lipsey, *Toward an Explanation of National Price Levels*. (Nov. 1983)
53. Avraham Ben-Bassat, *Reserve-Currency Diversification and the Substitution Account*. (March 1984)
*54. Jeffrey Sachs, *Theoretical Issues in International Borrowing*. (July 1984)
55. Marsha R. Shelburn, *Rules for Regulating Intervention under a Managed Float*. (Dec. 1984)

56. Paul De Grauwe, Marc Janssens, and Hilde Leliaert, *Real-Exchange-Rate Variability from 1920 to 1926 and 1973 to 1982*. (Sept. 1985)

SPECIAL PAPERS IN INTERNATIONAL ECONOMICS

8. Jagdish Bhagwati, *The Theory and Practice of Commercial Policy: Departures from Unified Exchange Rates*. (Jan. 1968)
*9. Marina von Neumann Whitman, *Policies for Internal and External Balance*. (Dec. 1970)
10. Richard E. Caves, *International Trade, International Investment, and Imperfect Markets*. (Nov. 1974)
*11. Edward Tower and Thomas D. Willett, *The Theory of Optimum Currency Areas and Exchange-Rate Flexibility*. (May 1976)
*12. Ronald W. Jones, *"Two-ness" in Trade Theory: Costs and Benefits*. (April 1977)
13. Louka T. Katseli-Papaefstratiou, *The Reemergence of the Purchasing Power Parity Doctrine in the 1970s*. (Dec. 1979)
*14. Morris Goldstein, *Have Flexible Exchange Rates Handicapped Macroeconomic Policy?* (June 1980)
15. Gene M. Grossman and J. David Richardson, *Strategic Trade Policy: A Survey of Issues and Early Analysis*. (April 1985)

REPRINTS IN INTERNATIONAL FINANCE

18. Peter B. Kenen, *Floats, Glides and Indicators: A Comparison of Methods for Changing Exchange Rates*. [Reprinted from *Journal of International Economics*, 5 (May 1975).] (June 1975)
19. Polly R. Allen and Peter B. Kenen, *The Balance of Payments, Exchange Rates, and Economic Policy: A Survey and Synthesis of Recent Developments*. [Reprinted from Center of Planning and Economic Research, Occasional Paper 33, Athens, Greece, 1978.] (April 1979)
20. William H. Branson, *Asset Markets and Relative Prices in Exchange Rate Determination*. [Reprinted from *Sozialwissenschaftliche Annalen*, Vol. 1, 1977.] (June 1980)
21. Peter B. Kenen, *The Analytics of a Substitution Account*. [Reprinted from *Banca Nazionale del Lavoro Quarterly Review*, No. 139 (Dec. 1981).] (Dec. 1981)
22. Jorge Braga de Macedo, *Exchange Rate Behavior with Currency Inconvertibility*. [Reprinted from *Journal of International Economics*, 12 (Feb. 1982).] (Sept. 1982)
23. Peter B. Kenen, *Use of the SDR to Supplement or Substitute for Other Means of Finance*. [Reprinted from George M. von Furstenberg, ed., *International Money and Credit: The Policy Roles*, Washington, IMF, 1983, Chap. 7.] (Dec. 1983)